TALES FROM THE OTHERGROUND

30 YEARS TENDING THE WORDROWS OF ELSEWHEN

POEMS BY
JOSEPH NICKS

Copyright © 2014 by Joseph Nicks
MagnesiumPieOtherground.com

ISBN 978-0-9831191-9-7

Published by Blue Jay Ink
Ojai, California
bluejayink.com

Book Design by Blue Jay Ink
Cover art and illustrations by D. Reeser

This is MagPie Book #16. Visit our website (The Magnesium Pie Otherground) for lists of previous (and forthcoming) titles dating back to 1983.

The 76 selections dated 2000 or earlier have previously appeared in other titles with a Joseph Nicks copyright, sometimes in a slightly different form.

The 26 poems dated 2001-2014 have never before seen the light of day.

This book is not to be confused with
Tales From The Otherground #9:
The Inverse Of "In" Verse
by Joseph Nicks © 1992

For Detroit – city of my birth,
on your 313th anniversary:
I hope you get back to feeling better soon.

For 50 years of Beatle songs and Mustangs.

For Martha, the last of her kind –
who died on the 1st of September, 100 years ago...

Chromonymous	8-9
April, Come What May	9
The Burning Leaves	10
Flux Factor	11
For That Which Almost Was	12
The Worker's Clothes	12
Better Wear A Helmet	13
Larvalous	13
Still Life	14
The Likes Of Me	15
If I Could Only Make It To The Moon	16-17
Bathyscape	17
Guerrilla Sunshine	18
Xenophilia	19
Simple	20
Ash Wednesday, A.D. 2002	21
1900 Friday	22
This Shit	22-23
I Walk The World	24-25
No Matter The Mercury	26
The Last Day Of That Year	27

Chromonymous

there's a place
in the film
where everything goes black
and white,
stark-naked as the printing
on the page

and if you care
to read it,
it can show you things
no colors can obscure

there's a place
in the painting
where the water colors
everything it touches,
cleansing every hue
of its distinction

to de-prettify the picture
as the pigments run together:
sky to grass
and trees to sea;
bricks to fog
and flesh to soil –
though their shapes
may still define them,
i'd almost rather have
the thousand words

there's a place
within the music
where the words
have made their nests
and weave between refrains
with guerrilla clarity;
subjugated by musicianship,
i'd almost rather sing them
for myself

19 August 1999

April, Come What May

the March was long and tortuous,
our ranks thinned by the day
and, April, green and foolish
with a thousand things to say
that blossomed into fever,
come what May –
we blessed each other
joyfully and sneezed:

again, again, a thousand times,
the tears run down our summered cheeks,
we danced upon the fields
and the fruit beneath our feet;
as ignorant as bliss,
unsorrowed as the dead
and dizzy as the water
down the drain

22 March 1988

The Burning Leaves

when summer's fat leans
toward the fall
and time and pulse
have quickened in the air;

when restless trees
are whispering
in urgency and eloquence
that knows no particular tongue;

when birds and sky
have gathered
for the distance,
i come home

and linger for a moment,
some two thousand miles away:
i'm not from around here
but i *was*

and now the burning leaves
enflame the trees
they've yet to take their leave of,
setting fire to the woods before they sleep

and now the burning leaves
me: emptiness, a withered hull
of would-be damage done,
my convictions acquitted all too soon...

05 October 1992

Flux Factor

people become people,
roads turn into roads,
and air escapes into the air –
i've seen the iron of these gates before
and i won't rest until i feel the way they felt
another time, another place
when i knew not so much as now
and i won't rest until i get that feeling down
and down in words

and, looking down another hill
onto another afternoon,
you'd think that i'd have seen this all before

but either i wasn't paying attention
or else i just didn't understand
because it escapes me even after all this time
01 December 1986

For That Which Almost Was

like a frantic, sweeping scrape
near the top of a prison wall
where the last escape attempt was foiled –
beautiful because of the freedom
it aspired to and almost achieved,
yet so disturbingly, tragically ugly
because it ultimately failed:

my nights belong to tearless desperation,
persisting in these last few gasps
of nearly non-existent atmosphere
where one can scarcely breathe another word
10 August 2000

The Worker's Clothes

no matter what the colors
you aspire to or are,
it only matters
what you do or don't;
whether you work
or let the others do it for you –
and that is why i wear the worker's clothes
so you'll make no mistake...
22 November 1997

Better Wear A Helmet

this hardened hungriness will drive me
all the way to Hesperia –
though it's a sixty minute ride
at seven thousand rpm
and the night is feral and frigid;
well they got a couple places there
where women will befriend you
for awhile…

and, though i'd really like, someday,
to understand the weather –
for now, well, i'll just feel it as it comes

16 November 1997

Larvalous

if i had a caterpillar,
i might watch it climb
the twigs and leaves
inside a mason jar

i might wait a long, lone winter
for the chrysalis to burst

i might cup my hands around it
while i stood there in my door way
and released it into springtime

if i had a caterpillar,
i might level this whole town,
crushing cars and toppling buildings,
slowly making my way home –
slowly making home my way

sometime 1985

Still Life

if there's still life,
there ought to be a spring
and, for once, we ought to take part

if there's a prime,
we ought to live that long
and if we already have,
we ought to at least remember
something of it

if there's a new order
resurgent among us,
there ought to be legs left to stand on;
if there's anything left worth dying for,
it ought to be worth living for 'til then

if there's a promised land,
it ought to be somewhere this side of the clouds;
it ought to be our promise to ourselves

if there's a warmth
to shake off our shivers,
the only way to spring
is through the winter

16 December 1995

The Likes Of Me

even though i live on Nowhere Street,
can it really be that bad?
got a job
and my own apartment
and i guess i should be glad

even though i'm going nowhere
faster than i ever did,
got a motorcycle
and a '68 Mercury
that can keep me off the skids

> odd though i hate everything,
> i love to go out walking
> to remind me why that is

even though i've grown more
meaningless than i ever was before,
got a girl and a handful of good friends –
who could ever ask for more?

even though the likes of me
have dwindled in dislike,
got generations come behind us
that we've got to pave the way for

> odd though i'm not happy
> about always being sad,
> just realizing i don't *need* to be happy
> has been the greatest dose of freedom
> the likes of me could ever receive

21 September 1997

If I Could Only Make It To The Moon

the sun, like hell-fire on high,
standing still and straight up
in the blistering blue aboveness
of evaporating air

the pavement, burned clean of all shadow –
not a precious drop of darkness to be had
in all the shallowing belowness of the land

the substrate and the firmament alike,
held captive by a tilt of 23.5 degrees
in the direction of the local star,
now basking in its prime

though its days, too, are quite ordinarily numbered
at five billion x three hundred sixty-five –
by then the very last of us
will long-since have been buried
in the frozen fossil book

'til then, there seems no real refuge
from the heav'ly-laden heat
among the homely or the homeless
all across this builderness,
the dues of which too soon again come due…

if i could only make it
to the wintering of day:

when the moon ascends to take its place
within the welcome darkening of sky

when shadows come out of hiding
to interact with scattered light
and distances are richened in the day-worn cityscape,
infused anew with thickness and resolve

when all the world comes tossing
and turning in and out
without a wounded thought
of surrendering to sleep

if i could only make it to the moon...

12 Jul 2006

Bathyscape

i went out into the desert
to bury my old self –
it took me some few years
to dig the sullen rock
and shifting sands

and it was lonely in the ground,
but for the winds
and the sunset
and the stars

i went out into the desert
to bury my old self –
and in the seventh year
i sprang anew

from the same old roots
no one of us escapes

25 June 2014

Guerrilla Sunshine

i know it's been a long, lean, narrow night –
as long as half our lives have been;
as lean as winter's fruit;
as narrow as the road wound through these woods

but somewhere on that morning,
sly guerrilla sunshine shone
in glints of here and there
amongst the gath'ring thunderhead

i know it's been so long since we've believed –
so long since we could breathe
half-hearted utterance of hope
for all the promise of The Worn-Out Word,
the teetering technology,
the gaping holes in hyped humanity

but somewhere in my reading,
i recall a stirring passage
in the fluttering of pages
on a hill

i know it's been a long time since the thaw
our frozen hearts and fingers
must have felt an age ago –
before the spring recoiled
beneath this seeming permafrost

but somewhere in the melting,
dripping deep inside of me,
i swear i glimpsed an errant ray
of warm guerrilla sunshine
gleaming ever-cautious
from somewhere between
the mountains and the clouds

19 January 1996

Xenophilia

somewhere in the 2nd grade,
i looked over at the picture
he was painting of the world –
the colors and the promise
of what "someday" might yet be
all seemed so much more plausible
than the smear i was concocting
and i just had to say to him
"i like yours better than mine"

and after many more years,
well, i looked up at all their lives –
the doubtlessness and fit
of everything they'd said and done;
the way they seemed to sleep
so easily and deep;
and i just had to say to them
"i like yours better than mine"

something she must've been saying
caused me to look over, then down
at how it was she filled the seat she sat in
and i just had to say to her
"i like yours better than mine"

ain't that what makes this old world spin;
what's got us in the mess we're in –
each other saying to each other
"i like yours better than mine"

?? April 1997

Simple

though i wouldn't trade this
for the simpleness
of those more simple-minded days
of breaking youth,
it really is
the simple things i miss:

like walking down this street
and simply walking down this street
without all the excess baggage
these years have obliged me to carry

like saying, "hey, good morning!"
and not having to stop and wonder
if it's true

like sitting down to eat
and contemplating no more
than chewing and swallowing
instead of all it took
to bring these things to my table

like lying here
in the still of the night –
in the depth of the night
and the breadth of the night
for the entire length of the night,
and not feeling so compelled
to try to mark such fathomless dimensions

04 October 1997

Ash Wednesday, A.D. 2002

four-thirty in the afternoon
in a warm and spacious room –
i'm spending some time
with my parents:

one sits waiting for the next friend
or relative to wander in

the other reclines peacefully
in a half-open box

outside the snow comes swirling,
ghost-dusting the black nakedness of trees;
i feel it now –
like never before,
the way she always said it got into her joints

i watch her,
now so shiverless...

and i resolve to never welcome
fickle warmth of any kind,

knowing now of not a god
who mitigates mortality
in some hypothetical hereafter –
despite heart-broken centuries
of threadbare reassurance,

i refuse to mute the mourning
with some heavenly-haloed hoax
of half-assed hope

26 February 2002

1900 Friday

i stood by
my evening window
and watched the weather change –
the traffic's never been a friend of mine

and, every once in awhile,
i feel like i'd like to remember
what it felt like to feel like shit

but how can you remember
what you cannot, first, forget?

07 February 1998

This Shit

it's all right here for now –
this shit belongs to me:

my wind

my moon

you can't take them away from me
any more than i can take them away from you

and, until it goes away again –
until the wind dies down
and the moon is swallowed up
by the skyline of the city,
i've got hundreds of hectares to hike across
and thousands of thinkings to think

like how all this shit happened
and somehow continues to

like how i can't get up
on top of it all
and yet how i refuse to go down

like how, in any given bar on any given night,
you can stumble across those life-affirming things
in conversation with a stranger
or the way the music turns –
or you can shake your head to hear of things
that spell the *ends* of lives:

car meets motorcycle at 65 miles an hour

stalker meets ex-fiancé
out front of the latter's new apartment

two boys whose britches got too big for them
meet each other in the parking lot

but after you step outside again
and the night blows over you,
this shit just takes its place
in anything and everything out there...

...and the hours left to get some walking done
02 December 2006

I Walk The World

i walk the world
in quasi-nausea,
unwilling to disgorge
the very things that poison me,
with the stubborn reasoning
that i'll finally wake one day
to find myself, despite myself, immune

i walk the world
in simmering resentment
of all that they
have forced me to become
just to grudgingly maintain
my marginal footing
in the slippery circumstance
of fleeting hominid advance

i walk the world
in slow-fermented guilt
for every cause i've failed to effect;
for every protest gone unlodged;
for each neglected chance
to punch them right between the eyes;
for every dozenth cheek
i've ever turned

i walk the world
in wonderment
of which i fear the most:
what they may, one day, do to me;
what i may, one day, do in turn to them

i walk the world
when wakedness wins, once again,
the war it's waged on sleep

most of all,
i walk the world
bent low beneath
the ponderous pall
of staggered and smothering sorrow
for every living thing
that's ever come unlived

14 October 2012

No Matter The Mercury

when the winds have finally subsided,
having hewn the lifeless landscape down
to wood and sand and bone;

when the diamonds in the sky
connive to pierce the icy blackness
of the very air that freezes in your throat;

when not a single drop of water
is quick enough to trickle into
lean liquidity;

when the longest night of the waning year
is still 12 days away;

when the last of your inner heat
has escaped into the frozen atmosphere;

do you stiffen in your steps
as inertia and viscosity
creep into every tissue?

do you shiver in futile resistance
to the onslaught of the frost?

do you swear you still can't feel
what isn't there?

because the cold, as we all know,
is only an absolute and utter absence
of anything at all...

09 December 2013

The Last Day Of That Year

as i sail along December streets,
grease-hued slush splatters virgin snow
like regret belaboring hope
and i feel the coming of age-old age
in a way i never have

but my driving leaves me weary
of my usual Janu-wariness
and as my motor drones into the darkness
of those last remaining hours,
i can't say i'll be sorry
to put that year behind me finally

and, though the road
on rubber tires
me, and i'd like nothing
more than rest,
i won't welcome my next recline
amongst the death that lies
so close beside the sleep

31 December 1995

VOLUME 2   ON THINGS I KNOW LITTLE OR NOTHING ABOUT ANYMORE

At My Age *(under the yoke of over)*	32
Bookend #2	33
Little-Read Book	34
Statistically Insignificant	35
Antarchitecture	36
The Scheme Of Things	37
A Brief History Of Windows	37
The Magnetic Field #2	38-39
Long Dist(urb)ance	40-41
Animals And Words	42-43
Movement 101	44
Pard-on	45
Vapor Chase	46
A Number One Than Yesterday	47
Beyond Belief	48-49
Gorilla^2 *(a Noah count poem)*	50-51
Recap	52-53
Tissues In Eternity	54-55
Something #1	56
Bookend #1	57

At My Age
(under the yoke of over)

once upon a time and twice upon a place;
three times i've started over,
slate wiped clean
and words lain waste

but the dust
of lessons lingers
as a haze upon the board
and a few brave cursive strokes
survive the reach of the eraser
as if to silently lend echo
to the murmuring of memory
in otherwise empty chambers

31 December 1995

Bookend #2

...i tried my best to salvage
what was left of the library,
but i couldn't save The Bible –
that most arrogant of books,
sworn on by a stack of its fellows
that its words were somehow
more than words –
that i should read them as if
they came from some higher source
than all the other words
of all the other volumes ever written;
that within its mortal covers
lie the elusive breath of God
as breathed through *only* these few authors
of all of those who've ever breathed a word...

29 March 1998

Little-Read Book

i just got out my little-read book
the evening that she said goodbye

i went from A to B,
i turned my ear to every def-
inition

there weren't no word
in my little-read book
to help describe the way i felt

but as the morning came around to C,
i saw the strangest thing:

ha, there was me at the kitchen table,
leaping from entry to entry;
spellbound by the guidewords
with nary a thought of a mere glossing over

like a fly entangled in a webster's snare;
G it's great to see you H and I
forgot her right away

and though i may get up to P
a little later on tonight,
i may not yet be quite on Q tomorrow morning

but i'll press on regardless
with the hope that someday soon
i may begin to see the Ys

sometime 1985

Statistically Insignificant

neglecting air resistance,
i skated down the freeway
ignoring friction

assuming ideal conditions at STP,
i stopped to check my oil

it was 7 AM,
Eastern Standard Time –
we were lining up
for The Normal Distribution,
my best friend hung himself
with a rope of zero mass
and i could feel my own resistance
buckling underneath the toll of bell-
shaped curves

11 February 1988

Antarchitecture

to tell the truth, i lie
awake with weary women
on my mind;
not a one that wouldn't slap me
if she caught me
thinking of her quite that way

to plumb the depths, i rise
about a quarter of
the moon;
not a dream i care to dream of
if it means i'll have to lie
down more than one more time again

to color life, i'll dye
my genes the fleshtones
of the dead;
no more than pigments
of their imagination,
so typically phenotypically
handed down

19 August 1994

The Scheme Of Things

and some will always come around
to suspect that there is nothing
in the darkness but the darkness,
which is still more than enough
to fill the pages of a life-
long dissertation on the subject;
though, in the scheme of things,
it really doesn't seem to matter
if any of it matters
but the scheme of things, itself

13 November 1997

A Brief History Of Windows

a few hundred years ago,
windows were always open;
until we invented a way
to see through them while they're closed –
we called it glass

which just may be
the most insidious substance
ever discovered –
just ask any bird

there's nothing colder than a window
when you're trying to find a warmth
beyond the pane

there's nothing harder than a window
when you can see
but not get through it
to someplace other than here

16 December 1992

The Magnetic Field #2

it draws me out my window
as i sit deskbound expounding
on some aspect of the actual
reduced to words and figures
i look up

to see beyond the field guides;
the field stands alone,
doing what it's always done
with/without our records and statistics,
specimens and specifications;
enduring introductions of exotic interlopers
and terrain-twisting implements
that have long-since gone to rust

was their iron drawn magnetically
to prove their shiny mettle on the soil?

did they just come down
from the trees to take the field?

it draws me,
the magnetic field –
so long ago fragmented,
still it draws my struggling conscience
far afield
of these warmed-over second stories,
jogging in me memories
of things i've never known –
etched upon the protoplast
some thousand thousand years before my name

it draws me,
knowing all too well –
in spite of all regrets,
that we'll be reunited in awhile...

09 October 1994

Long Dist(urb)ance

(i) Rainy Day Burrito

just a poorly-wrapped burrito
on a grey and rainy day
and the mercantile muzak
swirling through the soggy air
only served to spur remembrances
of why these damned Decembers hurt so much

i want to topple these traditions
in a decommissioned avalanche
of centuries-done-wrong;
come down like clouds unburdened
by the customary costumery
of "hip"-ocracy on high;
brought low to crush the cutting edge
and let it lie where it's been lying,
smothered in the rubble
of stale new ways of looking,
but not at...

(ii) Good Looking

and i had wished them all good looking
as i motioned to the mountain
and the telescoping glass
hanging half-unholstered at my hip
but, much to my syrup eyes,
they all ran home to looking good
instead of looking at...

(iii) Freeze Frame (December 1972)

all at once, all sight stood still –
immotional-cryogenic;

time frozen out of space
and fallen like mercury droplets
or rolling water in the dust

i realized right then/there
all my happiness had been had,
and so had i for having *had* it...

(iv) Alight in the Distance

having fled the sole proximity
of anywhere near myself,
i set out to melt these distances
in metric sleight-of-hand
while cycling over and over
the wheeling penumbra of Earth,
hoping at long last to land on the horizon...

(v) Circa 360 (actually 365¼)

how many ornery afternoons
await the long-spun
deepening of day
as it dissolves
into the darkness
of another blind-drawn night?

how many more mornings
must we endure
the shallowing of the world,
precipitating out of the waning darkness;
these claustrophobic landscapes
gaping so grotesquely grey,
asquirm with hominism and its ooze?

16 December 1996

Animals And Words

i looked up,
the sun looked down;
a good day for a ride
but the traffic wasn't mine
so i went back to work

i looked around,
the sky was there;
good day to write a poem
but the verse didn't stop
by here today
so i just wrote a check
to the water,
to the phone,
my landlord and the state

i took apart
a favorite song
to see why i liked it so much,
only to find i didn't
so i put it back together;
now it's fine

i woke up
the neighborhood;
good day to fall in love –
and i really wanted to,
but there weren't nothing
to fall in love with
so i picked up my wrenches,
walked downstairs to my garage

and in the late night radio,
i came to realize
that all that's left is words;
what's happened to all the animals
we used to pretend
not to be numbered among?

13 March 1988

Movement 101

do the tracks lain down
upon the ground
dictate the gait
that laid them down?

is a river
more the water
than the way that water flows?

can the wind be still
and still be called the wind?

how much of living
loses itself
in the space between
what's touched
and what is felt?

13 September 1997

Pard-on

i am not the lion
bellowing in the clearing
amongst his fellows
and his harem
as if to cower
all the savanna;

i am more the leopard
going silently and grudgingly
through the day and underbrush –
on his own
and on his way
back to the night;
the night from which
he emanates;
the night which
he eventually rejoins

23 April 1997

Vapor Chase

ice is not water
and water is not steam

and even though ice
seems to be the realest of the three –
frozen as it is
in solid absolution,
it is water
that makes rivers flow
and steam
that drives locomotives

deeds are not words
and words are not intent

and even though deeds
are the most concrete of the three –
standing there so clearly
in their tangibility,
it is the verbal flow
that incites, directs, explains
these doings
and it is the resolve
that initiates everything...

14 April 2001

A Number One Than Yesterday

do you know the bare of trees,
the frost of breath in air?
do you know the sling of salted slush,
the muffled crunch of footfalls on the shoulder?

do you know the Jesus Christ songs,
the peal of the distance in the bells?
do you know the moon of snowfields,
the stars of diamond cold?

do, you know – i do, you know;
not only that, i did;
did, you know – i did, you know;
before i even knew

do you know degrees of windchill,
the Christmasless, now-January winter?
do you know the shrouded silence,
the doorslam of the echo through the houses?

do you know the grey of skysteel,
the frozen flow of water down itself?
do you know the early sundown,
the pastel bleak of pink behind the trees?

do you know
the more you know,
the less you think you know?

do you know?
the more you know,
the less you think,
you know...

01 January 1996

Joseph Nicks

Beyond Belief

in the post-war era —
if we ever make it there,
what's left of us will doubtless
be some miles beyond belief,
out on the feral roadways
and walking off the distances
to measure what's been lost,
which may turn out to not be much at all

once more, that cemetery feeling
has come to comfort me —
everyone will be there soon enough
so why make such a fuss?

why not just settle down to living
and let the others living live;
stop striving to trade what we hold in our hands
for something we can't even see?

yeah, that cemetery thinking's
rolling peaceful over me;
a couple decades more or so,
i, too, will be beyond belief
and onto something more demonstrable

there's really no shame in admitting
you've not yet come to understand
what you earnestly try to wrap your mind around

but pretending you have answers
handed down here from on high
or filtered out of someone else's
hand-me-down translation
of translation of translation
of divine-claimed inspiration
is perhaps the most dishonest stroke of all:

if we could get beyond belief
and back to down-to-Earth confusion,
we might just grow some understanding on the way
17 July 2006

Gorilla^2 (a Noah count poem)

it must've gone something like this, at first:
Bison^2
Hyaena^2
Rattus^2
Lynx^2
Vulpes^2
Meles^2
Alces^2
Lutra^2...

but soon he must have found
that very few creatures
are so easily squared
away (in the taxonomic sense):

identifying (let alone finding 2 of)
every species of *Myotis* or *Crocidura*
was, no doubt, a major headache in itself

should he consider red-shafted and yellow-shafted
flickers to be members of the same species –
or should he take 2 of each just to be safe?

he'd have to take more than 2
wildebeest, elk, and harp seals
if he was planning on taking
lions, wolves, and polar bears
who aren't very fond of oats and alfalfa
and millions of earthworms
for the moles, salamanders, and robins,
not to mention billions of termites
(who could cause major problems on a wooden ark)
for just a few species of anteaters, aardvarks/wolves,
numbats, pangolins, and bat-eared foxes

let's see, if there are some 4400 species of mammals,
nearly 9000 birds, around 7000 reptiles
and almost 4000 amphibians,
he'd never get past the vertebrates,
much less the staggering number
of terrestrial arthropods
(thank God the 20,000+ species of fishes can swim!)

then there are all those animals
in the western hemisphere, whatever *that* is

and what of creatures like good old *Gorilla*^{2},
who wasn't even discovered
until well after the turn of the (19th) century?

well, a pair of them must have heard the news
and stowed away
because everybody knows gorillas can't swim

sometime 1984

Recap

you can measure it
with your calipers
and calculate
its cubic capacity

you can map
its fissured hemispheres
and label its topography

you can probe its infrastructure
with your circumspectral
radiant array

> but there are dimensions
> deep within that defy
> both space and time

you can hardwire it
into your gauges
as if this will somehow
measure its potential

you can place computers
conceived within it
on the starting line
right next to it
as if to mimic it
is to understand
the ways in which it works

you can even turn
the very thing
that does the thinking
back upon itself
in vain attempts to think out
how it thinks

      but this would be
      like tracks in the snow
      trying to tell
      the feet where to fall

you can unplug
all its connections,
microtome it into giblets,
extract its active ingredients,
and assay its chemical composition

      but you can't dissect
      its thinking,
      filter out what it imagined,
      or distill those things
      it saw and smelled and heard

04 October 1997

Tissues In Eternity

like tissues in eternity,
semi-formalin preserves

like the once-living
now on ice,
forever germ-and-shiverless;
potential energy conserved

like all the parts *in situ*,
trapped forever in their prime;
no hist'ry or experience
to build upon that time

like an ageless perfect specimen
incapable of growth/degeneration,
metabolically inert,
perpetuated now *ad infinitum*

like engines in antiquity,
now sparkless inexplicably
in spite of tireless dead reckonings
at roadsides, cages, mortuaries,
basements of museums:

poring over every pore
from sponge to *sapiens*,
bacillus to baleen;
expatriate biologists
exiled to the necrosphere –
in contemplation of the living,
we have walked among the dead
and grimly undertaken
such an inquest

do others wake these nights as i do,
frankensteinian futility enfevering their sleep?
09 November 1997

Something #1

there's something in the morning
that incapacitates the night
and spills your life's forgetfulness
across the breakfast table

there's something in your pocket
that could help you change the world,
but for better or for worse
is what you can't know 'til you do

there's something about a junkyard
and the history it belies
beneath the gaping hoods,
behind the torn-out backseats,
time of death
spelled out in frozen digits
to the nearest tenth of a mile...

there's something in the basement
and i heard it late last night
but i would sooner go to Hell
than go down there to see
what i would doubtless see

06 April 1987

Bookend #1

a book
about books
being eaten by bugs
was being eaten
by bugs

17 December 1986

VOLUME 3 THE ELUSIVE LIVING ROOM

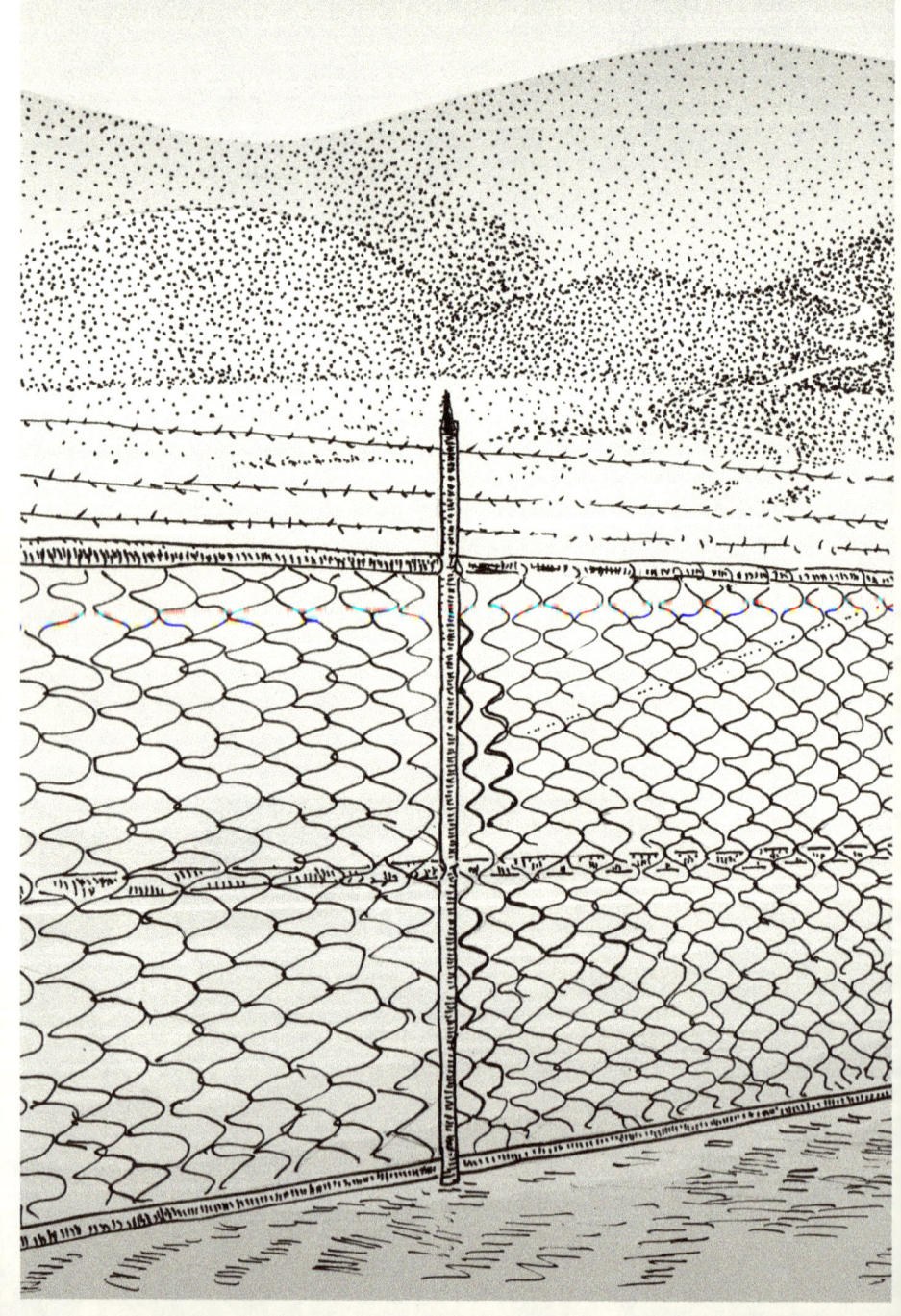

Ghost-Steps In The Dust	62
Time-And-A-Half	63
And None For The Days Of Not	64
Stillworks	65
Entrenched	66
News(worthy)	67
Origin	67
Zewmowt	68
Vangi's House	69
Parting	69
Away The Sky	70
Because It Only Lasts So Long	71
Midnight, Thirty-Eighth	72
Not Everything Is Dead Yet	73
Except The Hours Spent	74-75
And In The Wake Of Sleep	76-77
I Go To Hell #2	78-79
Suburban Purpose	80-81
If I Could Only Touch It	82
The Elusive Living Room	83
Reptime	84
Whisperless	85

Ghost-Steps In The Dust

down in someone's darkened basement –
dust some-dozened seasons deep,
having settled on the past
that's settled on the past
of stratified
life-long labors
in chaotic disarray:

how could anyone have told
when last someone had been there?

how could anyone have turned
such heavy pages?

05 October 1992

Time-And-A-Half

my dad had a back
that nothing could break –
not even 33 years at the plant;
the house is paid off, now,
he waters the lawn
and washes the car,
his back still intact
but something far deeper is broken:
the remembrance of what all that work was for

my mom had a dream
that no one could touch –
as it turned out, not even her;
she still gets up early
and works in the garden,
which is hers alone
until everyone else wakes up
and invades her world;
what saves her is the simple fact
that she always knew
it was just a dream

i can't for the life of me figure out
what made them want to have kids...

11 July 1988

And None For The Days Of Not

a clean shirt,
freshly-laundered
of the aura i impart to it
as i labor long to earn my daily bread:
one for each day
of having to go out into the world
and none for the days of not

a smiling face,
unfurrowed
by the thinking it can't belie
as i ponder so much more than bread alone:
one for each day
of having to go out into the world
and none for the days of not

a lightened heart,
unburdened
by the beatings of a lifetime
and the yearning to at last be hungerless:
one for each day
of having to go out into the world
and none for the days of not

23 May 2009

Stillworks

i felt the afternoon overcoming
all the spaces i reside in;
the darkness of the ages
was befalling me again

i looked up from the work
that loomed so difficult and large,
and i remembered:

every hope,
every belief,
every hard-earned dream
from liberty to lust,
every doubt,
every regret,
every sweat-hewn sculpture
toppling in the dust

the yokes we've labored under
have been mostly someone else's
for that is much of what there is to being human
26 April 1998

Entrenched

i like to put in a hard day,
lend my hand and make my way,
get off at last and make it home
in the evening–out of today –
i like to even though i always do

i like to climb up to my loft,
take out my pictures and my books,
put on my music,
think of all the other life forms
and places i should someday be –
i like to even though i seldom do

i like to look out my window,
forget the hopelessness and people
that surround me;
i like to relax and lay back,
so sure about the way the world should be;
i like to close my eyes and answer
all the questions here inside –
i like to even though i never do

18 June 1988

News(worthy)

the font from which
all print may flow
was rolled up
at my doorstep
like a Gutenberg
on kaiser roll
and i just couldn't wait
to see "what's happened"

'cause i knew it must be something –
things are always happening,
even when nothing is...

27 November 1997

Origin

up on the roof
in summer
with your hammer
in your hand,
nails gleaming
in the moonlight,
driven freshly
through the lumber
on a late
tar-papered night:

do the echoes
through the neighborhood
escape you now,
as then;
do you really forget
who you knew?

16 January 1986

Zewmowt

in the darkness of the day;
the sodden, blind obscurity
of milky-white midmorning
on its way to afternoon:

i can see the sun
for what it is
and that is just another star
surrounded, as they all are,
by the deep uncolored emptiness of space

i can see this race
for what it is
and that is just another species
basking, as they all do,
in the distant brave-sol burning;
the too-young-to-diurnal turning
of the world upon itself

21 March 2001

Vangi's House

sitting here
on Vangi's doorstep,
waiting for what may
or may not be

the lights are going out now –
one after another,
but still i feel the flow
as it surges through her pipes
and still i hear the wind
rush through her curtains...

17 May 2009

Parting

this morning i looked down
upon the stiffness in the cedar shavings,
just an everyday occurrence;
yesterday, the day before
and floating upside down inside the tank
among the bubbles and filtration –
one too many trips to my backyard
and where they lie beneath the soil
and the chuffing of the shovel;

is it any wonder,
after all these lives and deaths,
that some of us reluctantly
resolve to live alone?

29 April 1988

Away The Sky

rain, so fluid cold,
come down on streets and rooftops;
come gushing from the downspouts,
down to scrub the soapless alley cleaner still;
relentlessly come down
on buttressed tiers of untold stories,
anonymous pane upon pane

stolen looks through deep blue windows
in the swirling leaden skies;
windows rare and closing
on regretful afternoons

years blown clean and sober
as the chances of a lifetime
driven darkly through the middle of the day:

i smashed the phone today;
smashed it with one of my last remaining fists

now i just sit here staring
deep into its fractured ringlessness

and i smile in spite of the sky

22 October 1987

Because It Only Lasts So Long

if twilight lasted hours
and the sunset took all day;

if deep and longing shadows,
evening's breath so rarefied
could hang there and arrest our thoughts

long enough to catch the gist of it;

long enough to then examine it at length
in the last remaining light;

long enough to climb inside of it,
to get over downtown's skyline
or the dancing of the darkness on the waters,
so crescentically englimmered
by the pastel-lapped last gaspings of horizon,

perhaps it wouldn't do these things to us,

perhaps it wouldn't be so far beyond our grasp

19 March 1988

Midnight, Thirty-Eighth

step out into
the fog-enshrouded
silence of a suburb
sound asleep

not a single
dog is barking,
not a single
TV blares,
not a single
motor droning
down the distant
boulevard

and on this thirty-eighth
of April,
guess it's about time
to start calling
it May

but "May"
sounds too much
like a promise
far more likely
to end up
"May not"

08 May 2000

Not Everything Is Dead Yet

to find peace
is to give up both hope
(and its counterpart anxiety)
and regret
(the flipside of nostalgia) –
i wonder if it's possible to do this

when you have no preconceived expectation
of what's supposed to be,
the road is more important
than any single destination

when you're out to see what's out there
more than simply to "arrive":

though most of what's lived is no longer alive,
not everything is dead yet;

though the inevitability of it
is so hard to put out of our minds,
not everything is dead yet;

though i doubt we'll see the ones again
already gone away,
not everything is dead yet

so i suggest you get on out there
and live among the living while you can

23 May 2009

Except The Hours Spent

i didn't mean to live this long –
it's just something that befalls you
when you're not looking

and, though death is an idea
i most strenuously object to,
i can honestly say
i regret every day of my life

except the hours spent
with eyes to page,
hungrily vacuuming up
the words of wisdom
few and far between,
yet teeming in the volumes
of all that's written down

except the hours spent
with pen to paper
in the half-hearted hopefulness
of luminous afterhours,
so steadfastly determined
to assuage my own afflictions;
to gather my own meanings;
to summon my own resolve
from all those scattered moments
i have stolen from myself
so as not to have to see them
squandered 'neath the yokes
of toil or sleep

except the hours spent
with boots to landscape,
beckoned once again
by all there is and ever was
to see and smell
and sounds that turn your ears
to the tune of the terrain
and the symphony of silence
rising up beyond
the soon-to-be-toppled
pillars of over-extended civilization:

in some ways i'll be sorry to see it go
for all that i have gleaned
from the lyricist/musicians;
from the naturalists, philosophers
and flickered light of darkened theaters;
from sober talks in drunken plots
with the belabored, disenfranchised,
and the few not so like you

no, i didn't mean to live this song
and i don't expect it to get
much better than it's been,
with all that's left to live up to
and all that's left to live down;
with all that's left to dread and to regret
except the hours spent

03 June 2013

And In The Wake Of Sleep

how can i sleep
with the night
all around me like this?

and this something –
these somethings –
squirming to get out
and into it again,
although they've never
really been

like a long, lean,
light-shunned shadow
cast upon the darkness
of the deepest, darkest night;

like churning blood
spilled in my heart,
how could
anybody know
or tell
the difference?

but still,
somehow i do…

how can i wake
with morning
smeared all over the place?

and that nothing –
those nothings –
come creeping in again
to smother me
and any dreaming i may have
forgotten to extinguish

like a sickly wash
of bile-hued paint
splashed all over the oozing,
pus-colored landscape;

like phlegm
on top of vomit,
how could today
possibly fuck up
what tens of thousands before it
already *have*?

but still,
somehow it does…

                              06 December 1996

I Go To Hell #2

in the middle of the night
in the middle of the bed
in the middle of the room;
in the middle of my tossing,
turning middle of my dreams,
i go to Hell
and even waking up can't save me now

in the middle of the street
in the middle of the block
in the middle of a run
i've no more than half-begun;
in the middle of the places
i had hoped, someday, to go,
i go to Hell
and getting there's the only way
i know to stop me now

in the middle of forgetfulness,
the middle of my lines;
in the middle of the picture
i was painting on the middle of the wall;
in the middle of today,
tonight seems so much closer than this morning;
i could lay me down here somewhere
in the middle of my life
and go to Hell

in the middle of the radio
and midway home from work;
in the middle of my sanity,
i scream it at the world
to let me go, you fuckin' bastards –
let me go;
let me take my life
and go someplace i know that i should go,
i go to Hell

09 May 1986

Suburban Purpose

i live uptown
and i hate my life;
i eat my supper
and i fuck my wife;
i read my nothing-news,
subtract my ads;
i await my weather
and forescore my sports

i drive my car
down to buy some gas
so i can drive my car
to work to make some more –
more money i can use
to buy more gas

i go to school to learn
to change the world
into something similar
to what it is –
i store my data
and amass my facts;
i quote my figures
and collect my grades

i go to a movie
and i hurt myself;
i come back home
and hurt someone else;
i stop by a bar,
don't want to hurt no more;
i go to Hell again
and slam the door

gonna have me a kid,
gonna teach him shit
and he'll be bitter
because of it

gonna raise me a son
who can join the fight
and he'll grow up
to hate his life...

30 November 1988

If I Could Only Touch It

stuck here in someone else's hours,
watching the traffic be traffic:
doing what traffic does,
going where traffic goes –
petering out and dying down,
awalk down someone else's avenues,
adust in auburn aftertones
of deserted afternoons

there's something wrong, here,
but i can't quite figure out
just exactly what it is:
something so profoundly wrong
it pervades the lengths of the landscape,
the entirety of the atmosphere,
the sunshine and the shadows
and the shapes and shades and sounds
of all the discernible world

i can see it all too clearly
'til i try to pick it out;
i can hear it all too plainly
'til someone asks me what it sounds like;
i can smell it every time
i try to breathe

i can feel it like the summer
beating down upon my back;
i can feel it like the winter in my bones;
i can feel it 'til i try
to take it in my hands,
like someone else's/ours
that we both know but can't explain

09 February 2013

The Elusive Living Room

there is an insulated emptiness
run through this hollowed house
like warmth unwarranted
and vital signs that point
in no particular direction

there is an early darkness
that pervades the afternoon
and swallows up what light
will brave the curtains

there is a murmuring of voices
that filters down the hall
as nearly ninety narrow channels
drown all thought of conversation

there is a friendless mem'ry laps
the shore of once-shared landscapes,
now abandoned one by one
in the passages of age

there is a gallery of living
hanging all along the walls
that documents the exodus,
now generations-deep,
in search of nothing more elusive
than a little room to breathe;
a little room to stand;
a little room to run;

in search of nothing more elusive
than a little room to live…

11 January 1996

Reptime

tomorrow i wake up
and kiss the morning
with a lifetime's-worth
of possibilities

tomorrow i take up
where i long ago left off;
take up the slack of sixty seasons
donated to a cause
without effect

tomorrow i wake up
to think on yesterday's crippled promise;
to ponder my former impotence;
to sigh with great relief to think
that that's all over now

tomorrow i wake up
but it's today

03 November 1987

Whisperless

in the dead
of endless night;

in the still
of worlds devoid
of other inhabitants;

in the solitude
of shadows standing motionless
throughout an hourless land;

most any sound is music
to the silence –
most any word is news
to pen and page

25 August 1990

VOLUME 4   OMINA GEAUNAU

Forever Endeavors	90
In The Tropic Of Unpunctuated Summer	91
The Prodigal Sun	92-93
Six Feet Down The Road	94-95
Things I've Learned Out Here	96
Omina Geaunau	96-97
Beloved Zinfandel	98
Eight Mile Sigh	99
A Day In The Days	100-101
Unsnown	102
Extantaneous	103
Willamette Nocturne	104
Drinking Michigan	105
Plumbing The Depths Of Night	106-107
Full Cycle	108
Vaguerance	109
Bone Against Bone	110-111
Pictures Of Life	112-113
Down Fall	114-115

Forever Endeavors

to arrive on the horizon at long last
after all the miles that have come to pass –
what a remarkable achievement that would be

to fall down upon untrodden snow
and revel in its white virginity,
stretching out as far as anyone could see

to sing the unsung heroes,
basking in their anonymity –
gone forever now that you have fingered them

to wake to meet tomorrow
just before it turns today –
isn't that what we have longed for all along?

to finally snap on out of it
and bring ourselves back to our senses,
at last to see the carrot for the stick

19 December 1993

In The Tropic Of Unpunctuated Summer

the ponderous interminality
of day upon day upon day
where the good life plays out
in the surfishness
of sea against sand against sea
and the horizon beckons
in all the ultimateless infinitude
of everywhere to go
but nowhere to arrive –
no milestones or landmarks
to be labored toward or pilgrimed onward to
in the forever-merge of celestial and marine;
the blue goes on to gobble up the blue

oh, how everythere is magnified/exalted
by the distances from here;
how everyone wants onelessly
to put their lonely pieces to the whole –
how long it takes to learn how to belong!

oh, how each fleeting instant is so hopelessly lost
in the ocean of eternity –
and how that ocean is no more
than the teeming drops that flow
throughout its spanless span;
there's only one eternity
but an anonymous infinitude of instants
in a steady stream no longer
than time and time forever unbegun

28 July 2012

The Prodigal Sun

some wear the sun a-shining
like the smiling kiss of fortune
warmly bathing morning's hopeful window sill;
somewhere a woman is waking
to start a day i'm only ending
some summertime away

some wear the children, smiling
like a reason to be living,
like a lifetime to give berth to;
some wear their fathers/mothers
like the heroes on the shelves above their beds,
running out to be what they would've
in perhaps another lifetime

somewhere she sends a message
across a breaking October sky –
a copper sun as cold as stone
that seems to smolder in the east
so far away from home –
that says i could be running to
instead of running from again

some wear it well enough alone
but me, i have no coat of arms – no ring
around the collar
and i hold nothing against the winter
but the shadow of a shiver:

the shadow of a doubt,
cast across the sidewalk
in late autumn's afternoon,
so subtly that i never stubbed my toe;
i have waded through it long,
long awaiting everywhere and when i've been

and, though i know it's just the light
playing tricks on twisting trees
who toss, in turn, to play their windy tricks
on the likes of me,
i know i'm only waiting for the lightness of my head
to drive the darkness from my eyes

27 June 1984

Six Feet Down The Road

and when we walked,
we walked without –
no inner piece was coveted
by us

and where words were,
we often weren't,
our dialogues transcending
all the onliness of audibility

when autumn got the best of us
as summer had the worst,
well we went off
and often even off of off –
we weren't afraid
to look the winter in the eye

and, six feet down the road,
we seized the season,
with the thought that we'd be walking down
those life-affirming things
so recently gone missing
in the running down
of these Americas

and, six feet down the road,
we stopped
and went again
whenever we saw fit –
ours was the passage
no one else had seemed to miss

storm after storm,
we had endured
out where the springtime
feared to tread –

and i swear, a time or two,
we almost found it

and all the "it"s we set out for –
not finding them was revealing in itself

now in the snow i make a nest of me
but, ever since he went away,
the hours eschew their destiny –
a day is just a day;
and any inner warmth i felt
escapes into the frigid air
with all i thought i had to say

but we were
six feet down the road
and, since he's gone,
i'm four foot short

now, there's a lifetime to live up to
and a hist'ry to live down,
and one may be as short
as the other one's been long

no, there is life beyond this living –
and death beyond this life;
it's up to each of us to choose
how we'll face the foregone

i got some family
way back there,
and maybe someday i'll be home
but it's still about another half-year's walk

and all the other half of the way,
i'll catch the weather report
'cause we were six feet down the road
and, since he's gone, i'm four foot short

15 December 1984

Things I've Learned Out Here

water is free
and drinking a lot of it
can help you *feel* less hungry

bread doesn't really go bad;
it just gets a little stale and, at worst, a little moldy
and can be had for incredibly modest sums
just because it's not fresh from the oven
(if you wait long enough, they'll even throw it out
and then it's yours for free)

edible fruits on ornamental trees
are free for the taking
if no one sees you picking them off

and after all these years,
i've discovered just how much
i like the sound of bagpipes –

and i like it a real lot

sometime 1985

Omina Geaunau

there is a winter
within the winter;
a woods in the middle
of the woods

there's an ocean
at the bottom of the ocean
and a pilgrimage you
swear you'll still make good

there is water running down
to the water running down
to the water lapping all along the coast

there's a path that leads you to
the path that leads you to
the road that finally heads out on the road

when the home stretch
falls far short of home
and you're your only next of kin:
don't you wonder
how few others have
been every place they say that they have been

they're gonna build
a bigger building
where a building, on a vacant lot,
once stood

there's a landfill
that has landed full of empties
that belong to someone
else's neighborhood

there's a town inside a town
within this anthropopolis
where indigenous is synonymous with ghost

where the blattids and the *Rattus*
and *Pediculus humanus* swarm
the plague-ground of their *Homo*philic host

when the life seems
so devoid of life
and living room is in decline;
don't you wonder
if there's anyplace
left worth escapin' to this time

20 November 2004

Beloved Zinfandel
*(me and Ernest and Julio
down by the schoolyard)*

in the shadow of a doorway
of a building someonce lived in,
i have read the plaster cracks
as i have turned, in turn,
to wring my thirsty hands
around your neck
and kiss your glassy orifice,
dreaming dryly drunk of something better
than the ripple in my head
that waves me warmly wistful
through a bottleful of songs we used to know;
and now we sing for different reasons,
having lost much of the meaning
though the words are tattooed squarely
on the walls of swelling lungs

and you may know –
but no, not me;
i'll never set my thinking free
the way i've seen it break our vagabonds
into shiverless forgetfulness;
pass the time and pass the bottle,
anticipating only sleep
because in these parts,
as the slogan goes,
a winter never quits;

it just goes on
to yet become
one or another hopeless season

sometime 1985

Eight Mile Sigh

riding July by the window,
the moon on the highway ahead;
1983 or so and time was there to kill,
although i chose to spare it, just the same

the ride would soon be over
but no sooner than the night
and i drew a long, cool breath back there;
the longest, coolest one
the time and Tucumcari would allow

last night, the wheels rolled me;
i was taken aback by the seats
until the wind and longing road
rushing headlong past the bus
commenced the winnowing of innocence,
some years, now, overdue
and, with my shoulder to the window,
i exhaled long and deep –
letting go at least
an eight mile sigh,
and gave away my sleep...

26 February 1988

A Day In The Days

From Old Woman Springs Road
in the far-beyond-dry expanses nine dozen miles
before the dawn, two-and-a-half hours
to the hopelessly-broken, defiled biotic sacrilege
that is The Imperial Highway droning across
the mutilated multi-motored crisscrossed
crepuscular concrete-cracked urbanity
enmired in the selfishly-spittled spray-paint-pissed
overpassage of what used to be life and lives...

Over and over the hours of wallowing
wearisome work that perpetuates the proliferant
pro-lifer-ant pompous pontification
of microsoftheaded and
apple-engorged vapidity;
the virtual ether-breathed utterances
of cybermoronic
but oh so smartphonic servitude
to a tonguelessly text-driven talk-box a-twitter
with meaningless mull:
the digital dumfounding of the democritudes
via the omnipresent opiate of over-advertised
accoutrements and affluences
and absolute-unnecessities
plugged by pusher-pimp PR people
through the relentlessly re-iterated reticulation
of worldwide webbage
and the bombastic bonappetitedness
of belching bourgeois bon vivants
whose mumbled maws gobble gratuitously
as they drool and slurp
and sleeve-wipe themselves on the camera...

Sailing The Gerald Desmond Bridge,
just shy of Vincent Thomas, and descendent
to the shipping lanes – the portage of Terminal Island
and the termination of terrestrial transportation:
here lies a sanded stretch sea-birded
in teeming tern replenishment
enhappening each annum
since perhaps The Pleistocene,
though recently relegated to remnants
of the all-engulfing anthropospheric annexation;
a few will fledge to fish anew if only unentangled
by the casting off of monofilament...

Back along the belabored bluffs
of Ocean Boulevard,
the sidled stroll of semi-solitude, still peopled
by a people predisposed to populate,
and up the steeps to Signal Hill
to delve into the dusk –
awhile away, the evening-out of all we are aware...

28 July 2012

Unsnown

you may sit by
your winter window,
waiting for the world to turn
your way

or

you may get up
and walk away;
a long and lonely way
across the nameless white expanses
from a life left too long-lingered in the lurch...

05 February 2014

Extantaneous

comes a time when time runs timeless,
when your time is time long past
and you come, at last, to realize:

that every epoch, era, eon
elapses as ephemerally as air into thin air –
millennia as gone as milliseconds,
momentary mountains,
instantaneous oceans,
the split-second spark of the sun

that no time has been less
(or will be more) important
than the hour now at hand –
early into late back into early,
sleep and wakedness
as arbitrary as activity and fuel

that any essence settles out
as dew upon the leaves
and trickles into soil,
percolating down through layer after layer,
the pages of terrestrial history,
perhaps to be peeled back
by some long-tomorrowed reader
immersed as temporarily as you
in these minute minutes lapsing
into fleeting memory

29 March 2013

Willamette Nocturne

spirits in the sky
like drunken breath
in autumn air,
lying down to take my rest
upon the frost
upon the leaves
upon a long, lean winter's doorstep

i was lost
in wood and shrubbery
and newfound as the night
set down upon the middle of a town
so tucked away
that streetlamps scarce
subdue the darkness
measured intervals away:

i was dead to the world
but never more alive
than those places in the mountains
grown so dark at night
you never have to even close your eyes
to find your sleep...

22 June 1988

Drinking Michigan

i got the grass is greener blues
an' i been drinking Michigan;
a week, a day, another dozen months
until i set foot on this soil once again

i got airborne anyway,
my afterberth left trails in the sky

i got over the landscape
just in time to come back down;
i got down

i got no time for money,
got no money for The Times;
i got no need for newness
and no news is good to me

i got to get up every mornin'
'cept that last one;
i got so god-damned many ideas,
they're startin' to get ideas of their own,
and i'm only gonna be needin' this poor old back
about another twenty years...

i got the grass is greener blues
an' i been drinking Michigan –
i'm just about a million miles from drunk

07 August 1990

Plumbing The Depths Of Night

just past three o'clock east
at Tucson in the morning;
marking the time of desert,
the dimensions of the hour
and the ephemeral eternity of terrain

nocturning rpms
droning on relentlessly
to intercept the dreaded breaking of yet another day
that yet another night
will be obliged to give repair to

the road, wherever rolling,
and its multi-varied noises punctuate the silent night
with the gear-whine and the wind
that would cease
but for our surge upon the stillness

tomorrow i'll square with my wheels
and pull off to get my bearings, grease my joints
with a quart or two of sleep
at a quarter past the peak
that's been looming long upon my downhill slide

but how can we measure tomorrows
that never see fit to befall us,
so inescapably, instantaneously todayed?

how can we retrieve a single yestermoment,
time's transmission only equipped
with forward gears?
and when does the clock stop ticking
to leave us forever unfutured
as the present makes peace with the past?

ask me when i wake some night
in a room some ages away

ask me if i make it there,
because 'til then there's still some driving left to do...
19 December 2005

Full Cycle
(the wind and longing road)

yes to day
and no to morrow,
i was up on two wheels again,
rethinking my long-standing pacifism
and breathing in between the broken lines

the night belonged to my bike
and the throttle belonged to me,
i belonged to the road
and the road belonged to the night –
and a week and a day and a half later,
The Everglades still burned in my eyes...

and every now and then
i look around
and find me in the now, and then
i know the wind
will blow full cycle
and around again
and all along the longing road,
longing for the last of this
and lasting all night long

and, out here in the middle
of my gas tank and the night,

"it really can't get any darker, right?"
i ask nobody there

27 February 1988

Vaguerance

peculiar as a Friday
in the balance
of the head and heart and hands,
i cast my busy thinking
out across these neighborhoods,
the autumn swiftly waning
as the daylight does in winter;
the chill descends
like dew upon my conscience

and on a late, late afternoon,
i settle in like the fog on a hillside
and distant dogs echo into the darkness
11 December 1987

Bone Against Bone

and i have cast my vacant lots for this,
the ghost of a chance of a once in a lifetime –
yours and mine and ours and theirs
and all the multitude among us and beyond us
at our cursive, overwarm, proximal best,
running blindly down to swell each other's ranks,
to crash as surly waves
upon the morning's concrete shore
and dash our soles against the curb
and cast our eyes into the cracks
that groan and buckle all around us,
stepping up and down upon the norm
as we lean into the bell-shaped curves
that never look the competition in the eye,
but feel their breath upon our necks
and their toes upon our heels,
running bone against dew-freckled bone,
running bone against bone against bone

and i have read the fossil record
by the lamp above my bed,
dimly lit against the ink of afterhours,
eyes strained from the solution
where the questions have dissolved
to precipitate my re-confessed confusion;
i've made these Cretaceous-not-so-Tertiary transits
up and back and, backin' up,
as yet no evidence refutes
these steeped conclusions –
no hyped and homegrown hunch-backed biblically
by nothing more than beaches strewn in disarray
of bone against innominate bone;
cast over the stratified powder
of bone against bone against bone

and we have wanted it so badly
that history repeats us,
far beyond our best intentions
as we mutilate the very things
we've softly sworn we love the most;
arms thrown around each other,
our imagination captured
as Johnny comes marching home
time and time again
from the spring into the fall
of bone against crunching bone,
falling one amongst the others,
bone against bone against bone

and i have loved you in the evening,
despised you in the dawn's repulsive light
where i vomit at the sight of you
and, gagging on the thought of our relation,
myself comes face to face myself,
i've learned to come around
and take us hand-in-hand
along the stony walls of conscience
to the warm, compassioned chambers
just a lifetime down the dumbstruck corridor –
where, punctured by the bony words
that growl so deep within our throats,
we've shattered the conspired silence
and exposed ourselves to the naked embrace
of bone against lonely bone,
of bone against bone against bone

16 November 1984

Pictures Of Life

in my eager younger days,
i paged through volume
after volume;
reading their descriptions,
examining their pictures,
immersing my imagination
in the stories
of the way each species lived

then out into the biosphere
i ventured with my mates –
at least the carved up remnants
that our suburbs would allow

in my squirming coming of age,
i drew closer in my pondered walks
from the museum to the zoo;
down the hallowed halls of intimate detail
and through the gardened air to watch them breathe
and move around

then out into the biosphere
i ventured on my own –
straining at the canned preserves
that staved off premature extinction

in my mid-aged resignation
still unsettled by my weakening resolve,
i drove kilometric distances across half-continents –
perhaps a hundred hours
each eight-thousand-houred year
with barely glints remaining
of all the splendid life forms
i might yet cast my lonely eyes upon

then out into the biosphere
i ventured in recall —
beyond the disappointment
of the circumstance surrounding waning life

in my faltering last decades,
i tap my reminiscences
like maple trees in winter —
remembering just how sapless
all these woods have really been

then out into the biosphere
i venture in regret —
for all the sacred places
of unvisited neglect;
i take out my would-be picture book,
imagining what life must still be like

09 November 2004

Down Fall

it's October
and i need to walk
because it's the only thing
i'm really any good at

though it's a stupid thing to say
because almost everyone can walk,
i mean to say i'm *really* good at it

in fact, if i might be so bold,
i'm probably one of the best walkers
in the world

and since autumn seems
to bring out the best in folks –
well, it's October
and i need to walk:

down along the gravel roads
and through their neighborhoods;
down upon the fallen leaves
and down into the woods

down beneath the bird-fled skies,
the copper, stony sun;
down among the flaming trees
and silver-frosted lawns

until these lingered, brooding weeks
relinquish to the winter all their colors –
until i find an alternate profession;
until i wake to crippled legs,
my feet are late for steppin'

and as autumn falls
with early dusk,
the lights aglow in windows
of the houses far below,
the hallowed moon ascends
to take its throne

i turn my collar into the wind
to catch the breath
of another year
before it sails

i set my feet upon the fields
and turn my thinking out
to do the thing that i do best –
it's October
and i need to walk...

27 October 1999

VOLUME 5   FIFTH DEMENTIA

Only For The Winter	120
Suspended Autumnation	121
You May Feel A Little Prick	122-123
If I Stopped	124
Between Seasons	125
Lament For Each Other	126-127
Rubber Sol	127
8:30 Monday Nigh	128
Homo Phobia	129
Hey Bulldog	130-131
Pot Roast	132-133
So Far Beneath The World	134-135
Somewhere, Anywhere, Everywhere/Nowhere At All	136-138
Eleventy-Leventh Lament	139
In The Mourning	140-141
Slope Intercept	142
Lasting	142
But First Will Be The Winter	143
Two Thousand Down...	144-145
Aren't You Happy??	146-147

Only For The Winter

bedamned but i still see it
though my eyes have long since turned
and cast their vision groundward
like an airplane's last low photographs
from just above and beachward,
hanging frameless in the frigid halls of air:

alone not lonely figures
some kilometers apart,
unhuddled and unshiv'ring
but never far from fire

as the afternoon goes early
in the deepening of day,
these burnings lume into the lightlessness
so as not to seem so far away

but then it never grows quite dark enough
to obscure the icy distances between
lain down some long, lean years ago,
thinking it was only for the winter

eyes have frozen open,
not a tear can make the passage,
not a blink beats back the winds

only dreams are sleeping
and Earth is growing old…

23 December 1992

Suspended Autumnation

in the black
of birded wings
against the hope
of skyless gloom:

i can grey
the flighted steeliness
of real against
the sleep –
the sleep that comes
so whetherless
of wakedness or not

i can dawn
upon myself
the breaking-after
newness of the mournings
left unfelt

in the smoldering
nov-embers
of impending dreadlessness –
the fountain of euthanasia;
all encumbrance
comes uncinched:

i can succumb
to every color
waxing autumnatically
soon to be relinquished
to the winter

31 October 2003

You May Feel A Little Prick

when i was 17,
it was a very good year
for somebody
and maybe lots of them, at that:

i sat down in a theater
among *The Grapes Of Wrath*
and i remember asking,
"this is going to hurt, isn't it?"

when i was 21,
and still no one,
i was worrying about a future
i had no reason to expect:

i walked along the riverfront
by afternoon and evening,
Nat "King" Cole,
and with the records dropping
one upon another
as the needle skated wickedly across,
i'm sure i can recall
thinking somewhere to myself,
"this is going to hurt, isn't it?"

when i was 35,
or maybe not just yet,
i can't imagine thinking
things were better:

i was standing by the road, i think,
most likely on my way out;
someone grabbed my arm
and as i turned again
i distinctly remember asking,
"this is going to hurt, isn't it?"

25 April 1987

If I Stopped

tonight through Smithson's Hardware,
like long-gone Christmases and dads,
the tools and tools and powertools
could overtake me in my tracks;
if i stopped,
i stopped for long enough
to quench my thirsty heart

tonight through streets and runoff
i have waded and the slush,
the words and words and passages
could cut me down to sighs;
if i stopped,
i stopped for longing –
nowadays i catch my breath

and now i crave that song like jelly
and i need that song like bread
but the weather i won't whimper
and the morning i won't beg

yet tonight through dreams of dreaming,
i remember how it was
when eyes and eyes and eyelids
could be closed upon the night;
if i stopped,
i stopped no longer
than it took to break my fall

29 September 1986

Between Seasons

birds have flown
and winds have gathered;
trees are naked,
days are numbered;
the sky seems shallower
and the sun much farther away

and all resolve is tested
by the bleak and barren
early resignation of the light
to the long, lean, frost-gnawed night
that seems to need no evening to commence

with autumn out of earshot
and winter weeks away,
all hope just dangles numb
between foreboding and regret
like lives unlived
and life unlivened
by the promises of spring

how many here must languish,
suspended between tenacity and repose
and those festering last hours
that stretch from death to burial;
so stone-cold, yet so warm with teeming life

11 November 1995

Lament For Each Other

it was easy to think the words would last,
so warm and tucked away;
it was easy to say "forever" then
in the same breath as "you and me"

but tramping through the outlands
of these harsher latitudes,
new words tumbled into our paths;
words like "thorn" and "stone" and "rain",
like "frost" and "darkness",
"sand" in boots and eyes

yes, it was easy to say "forever" once
in volumes of unspoken verse

but as pathways wound and twisted
through the aching wilderness,
our "always" turned to "usually"
and then to "every so often"

and gathered in the glowing warmth
of once-in-too-great-a-while,
when we happened on each other in the woods,
the light still danced there in our eyes
but somehow disconnected from the words

and nights we stopped to lie down alone
wherever each sunset saw fit,
wearily strewn there among our own tracks
like bones in the tunnel of love

and after all these years
we still hear of or from each other

and hidden sighs of resignation
punctuate the words

25 March 1988

Rubber Sol

in the sun,
i think of you
and it's OK – in fact,
it's very, very good;
although it's not the way i used to,
in the afternoon i find i think of you

and i miss you more than my car –
i even miss you more than my dog,
but that should come as no surprise
since i don't think either of them
ever missed you at all

sometime 1985

8:30 Monday Night

another hour and a half
and maybe i'll be all right;
i'll get up and close my books,
lay down my pen upon my papers –
it was all beginning to fade anyway,
and i'll go out into the darkened living room
and watch another chapter
in the Richard Kimble story

another night's tossing and turning
in whatever dreams still remain
and maybe i'll be all right;
i'll say my prayers and make my plans –
perhaps they'll still be viable by dawn,
though not so very likely anymore

another eight hours and i'll get off
and maybe i'll be all right
and be on my way home for awhile

another twenty years on the job
and maybe i'll be all right;
sit back, collect my pension
and busy myself in the backyard
of my almost paid-off home

another long lonely lifetime
and maybe i'll be all right
when they can close the lid
and lower away,
repack the earth
and leave me to my rest

17 October 1988

Homo **Phobia**

partridges circle hungrily above me
and mallards pick at my flesh

gazelles flock in the thicket
and stalk me in the open
and the hamster gnaws my bones

manatees circle and menace my boat
as shoals of voracious sardines
lurk just beneath the surface

the tortoise snarls
and butterflies howl for my blood

the hare leaps at my throat
and deer tear at my flanks

but, lo, i shall not fear
for God is on my side
and he will surely help me
to smite all mine enemies

01 April 2009

Hey Bulldog

wolf like a lap dog
and crow like a cock;
face like a mirror
and heart like a clock;
the world is big and round
and 'round us every day –
it turns and turns away;
each day sees new birth
and new buildings –
the work force is drunk on its ass

and the change, it comes in quarters
if it ever comes at all –
fiscal seasons tick away our interest in the night
come to punctuate the daze we sleepwalk through,
semester on semester,
learning lessens by degrees...

well i was sick that summer – real sick;
like a fever in my belly,
mourning sickness in my eyes,
and while the road was healing me,
old Dylan up and died:
another dog, another day

there's a patch in the garden, two-by-three;
they tell me that's where he lies,
but what am i to answer when the questions
don't come around here no more,
when all the news is no news at all,
and home just stops feelin' like home?
the Orange County sun sets so strangely;
the afternoon twists so queer
and the change, it comes in quarters
from a dollar-fifty beer

but when the traffic falls this way once more,
well, it's just me against the parking lot —
i punch up some '50s/'60s station
and ride out of this stillborn dusk
on a pink carnation and a pickup truck

hey, hey, little bulldog, i wrote you a song
'bout a lot of new things that've been all along;
hey old Dylan, though i'm reaching deep down,
i can't launch another lullaby or similar sound
'cuz i'm not sleepy
and there ain't no place
i'm going to

13 February 1988

Pot Roast

I used to call him "Pot Roast"
though his Christian name was "Champ".
He hated me for my hominism.
I despised him for his domestication.
(Or so we pretended.)
He tormented me with his nocturnal yeowling.
I ridiculed him for being
"a disgrace to the family Felidae".
And, after a week or two, i'd go away again,
not to see him for another year or so.

The rest of the family
just good-naturedly took it in stride –
this pseudo-feud we carried on for 16 years.
See, i left Detroit in 1979
and he sort of came along and took my place;
a spoiled little bastard, i'd always thought,
but underneath it all, i sensed,
a *bona fide* felid nonetheless.

I saw him just nine days ago,
this pot roast turned to spare ribs,
and marveled at how
"he'd lost two whole cats" since the year before
due to a malfunctioning thyroid gland.

He couldn't seem to sleep or stay inside for very long
(even though it was just above zero °F outside).
There was a restlessness about him
that upset the whole household…

My sister called this morning
to say that he'd be resting now
and i knew that, in the grand scheme of things,
it really didn't matter.

But waiting for my bus
in these first grudging signs of light,
my thinking steals down the highway
through the fog –
and all this (death and dying) still manages
to stick in my throat.

10 January 1997

So Far Beneath The World

my eyes wander wearily outward
to a westerly-fleeting horizon
erecting its dusk-frozen silhouettes
to a backdrop of last gasps of pink
losing sky to the deepening blue

what once took teen-aged breath away
now smacks of smug sunset cliché
and palm tree propaganda

twenty years, now,
and i still don't get it –
or maybe i don't even get
just what there is to get...

"don't go outside with naked eyes
in years as dark as these
to see the unembellished world",
they warned me, over and over again –
their deaf ears fell
upon my words
and ripped them all

to hell:

condemned to catacombed obscurity,
feebly scrawled upon these walls
and cloaked in a subterranean blackness
i must sightlessly feel my way through –
i stop somewhere along the petroglyph
that memory seems to serve;

i strike my last remaining match,
light my sad little stump of a torch
and begin reading the wordrows aloud:

ranting, raving, rising to a fever pitch
of unquellable madness,
resounding through the deep and dark
deserted passageways,
reverberating in oblivion

'til the last faint echoes trail off,
swallowed by the solemn rock
so far beneath the world

09 May 2000

Somewhere, Anywhere, Everywhere/Nowhere At All

(somewhere)

a single little cool white puffy cloud
hanging high in the burning blue sky
cut off from the rest of the cloud bank,
lain low upon the slopes of distant hills

the angry air has settled there
right now unbound for anywhere
in any kind of hurry

the panting birds, unfolded wings,
are hunched among the needled leaves
with little thought of song

the sand and rocks are shimmering
with radiated heat
and all that go upon the land,
from ground squirrel to lizard,
will venture only sparingly
into the glaring day

the streaming of the ants
belies a death march to the mound;
the very buzzing of the flies
is labored, less insistent

and everyone is waiting there –
waiting for a whisper in the wind...

(anywhere)

a single streetlight lights the street
upstreet of all the others
and casts its yellowed cape aground
to wash the grey concrete

in dimlit rooms of brave AM
long after the din has died down,
the glass-and-plaster overlook
of traffic jams ago:

the books in single file
turn their backs upon the room
'til each in turn is taken down
to unfold some distant corner of the world

upon the walls, the wanted ones –
wanted for inciting and insight,
look down upon the yearning labors
deep into the night,
weary but insomniac;
in vain but not-so-vain

the murmured music emanates,
reverberates through marrow,
out these windows,
down these streets

and everyone is waiting there –
waiting for a whisper in the wind…

(everywhere/nowhere at all)

a single figure stands straight up
from whence (s)he has knelt down –
the flowers all will wilt before the sunset,
come the moonlit marbled gleam

they gather midday, heres and theres
in black and veiled garb
while words of one drone outward
monotone across the campus
and the freshly-tampered sod,
begging for a sigh of punctuation

a better place gone on to is the promise
most still cling to –
or almost wish they did;
the rest resign themselves
to only what their senses ascertain
and hope against the hopelessness
for something to believe

but none has yet assured us
from that one-way lost-and-found;
from their boxes in the ground
or their ashes scattered roundly
'cross the landscape and the sea

remembrances weigh heavy now
as each turns in their turn
to make for home alone

and everyone is waiting there –
waiting for a whisper in the wind...

10 July 2011

Eleventy-Leventh Lament

i live in a broken house
on a broken street
complete with broken neighbors
who stagger home late from the broken bar
to contribute to my broken sleep

i stew in broken silence,
broken drive-by music
assailing broken ears
with broken language

i wake to broken dawn
and thread my way through broken traffic
on my way to broken work
i've always done for broken pay

i lie down on my broken back
amidst my broken living room –
i listen to the breaking news
screaming from the broken networks
in between repeatedly-broken commercial breaks

and, through my broken window,
i gaze out on a broken world
that stubbornly resists
the broken plans i've labored under
over forty broken years

and i'd get down
on my broken knees
and pray my broken prayers
but as i look up through broken eyes
into these brooding broken skies,
i notice even god is broken

15 September 1998

In The Mourning

last night i held you close –
as close as separate bodies
would allow

last night my eyes would close,
from time to time,
in dreams of what must be

and with my ear pressed to your breast –
plunged into premature regret,
i remembered my reluctance
to commit myself to kissing
more than just one life good bye

now two of us must die
instead of one –
two must mourn one more
among the ranks of those
already to be mourned

and in the mourning lies no wake
if one should die, for Jesus' sake;
no long-assured reunion –
mother-child
or lover-loved one,
boy-and-dog
or dear old dad;
what's gone is likely gone for good,
all brave, heart-broken hope
of happy endings shattered

and so i hold you
as we dream
the only dream
that can endure:
when the dust
that once was me
mingles with that
which will be you,
blown together in eternity
as, grain upon grain,
we come, at last, to rest...

        21 April 1998

Slope Intercept

in the deeper shades
of afternoon,
all things seem to hang heavier
and so much more real in the air

on the slope of a hill
that the wind washes new every day,
contradictions all come swirling
in the gist of how it is:

where hope salutes regret
and fear gives way to resolve

where foregone resignation
and long-shot possibility
somehow find themselves commingled
and all our sins forgive themselves
in grudging generosity

will death *really* be
more agony than relief?

        01 April 2009

Lasting

when the moon
bathes our bedroom
in parallel lumes
enshadowed by
half-blinded panes,

when the breeze
feebly tingles
the left-behind chimes
of some ex-neighbor's
vacant backyard,

when dreams flicker
in porpoising consciousness
while memory flutters in vain,

i reach across the ages
time has gnawed out of our place
to plainly feel
the emptiness beside me –

longing for the distance
that will fade
this all to nothing more
than vague remembrances

26 July 2000

But First Will Be The Winter

there may yet come a day
when vernal fragrance re-invades the wind;
when joints and rivers thaw
as warmth reclaims the landscape
and the white gives way to brown,
which, in turn, gives way to green
and steely grey disperses
in the face of broadened blue

there may yet come the summered songs
of branches both re-feathered and re-leaved;
of chorused ponds in cursive meadows,
the buzz of pollination
and the swarming on the fields;
of the fluttering of wings across the moon

there may yet come the golden, red
and yellow-flaming trees;
the gathered flocks and fattened sheaves
and denning in the ground;
the clashing of the antlers in the rut

but first will be the winter
and the long and leaden sleep;
the dying back of layer upon layer
of life and limb and livelihood –
of outer fat and inner flame, a-flicker in the wind;
the hewing away of tissues
as the cunning cold comes creeping
into hands and head and heart,
overcoming every cubic inch of you

29 December 2012

Two Thousand Down...

to retrieve the golden loneliness
i used to call my own,
unhaunted by the prospect
of living with me and *only* me
in the wake of all these shambles
my life has made of itself:

for this i'd trade security
and next of kin,
paid passage(s) to afterlives
the living must yield to

for this i'd trade the smothered warmth
of conditional belonging,
the squirming claustrophobic chance to be only
intermittently myself...

once i climbed the hills of days
my youth could not have numbered
and strained my ears to hear the godly somethings
i was sure were so important:

the drone of an airplane high above
on a deep blue summer's
lazy afternoon –
lazy with forgetfulness
of all uneasing thoughts,
for an hour – no more than an hour,
i swear...

and once i climbed the stairs of nights
my thirsty heart could not help feeling bereft of
as i threw my hungry gaze
far out across the weary skyline,
vowing by now-godless skies
that they'd sooner squeeze
the breath from these lungs
than knock this stubborn resistance out of me

deep into such deserted hours
as i swear no more
than twenty any-others were also awake in,
i made every imagined pilgrimage –
from Galilee to Liverpool,
Galapagos to Magellanic Straits,
Serengeti to Sea Of Serenity,
but this pilgrim made no progress...

i went walking in the winter night
and everything was dead –
not so different from how i used to walk
when things were still alive;
at the turn of another thousandth year,
not a living thing was stirring

31 December 1999

Aren't You Happy??

it was late in the evening –
the 24th of December back in 1976,
and the teeming snow was tumbling
obliquely, unhurriedly down
and blanketing the fields

the sky was still wide open, though –
and he persisted,
long after those of lesser faith
had all gone off to bed;
rocking back and forth
upon the spacious window sill,
all the while singing softly to himself

he was somewhere between 35 and 40 years of age
and i know it wasn't family he awaited
as his hopeful eyes still scanned the sterile skies –
the orderlies had told me that, like many there,
his family had stopped visiting many years ago

i said good-bye to my sister –
as always, never certain she even knows who i am

and i was nearly to the door
when three musical little words brought me up short:

"Aren't you happy??"

and as i turned into his beaming smile,
no leaden stoicism could've muted my response

"Of course – i can't *wait* until tomorrow!"

"Me neither! G'bye, now –
i hope you get everything you wanted!"

outside on the landing
in the swirling of the snow,
i had not a doubt
that, in that happy corner,
i'd just seen the saddest thing i'd ever see
as i closed the very last door
that stood between the happy and the sad –
and chose the side upon which i'd remain

24 October 1994

*Well, that's about it
except to say that
the contents of this book
would not be possible
without the collective influence
of the following:*

*The many and varied folks
whose paths crossed mine
at the JWPCP in Carson CA
from 1979 to 1994,
leaving their footprints
deep in my loam*

*My Long Beach comrades-in-arms
from the early 1980s,
most of whom
are still with me
to this day,
lending music to my years*

*The few who fought the good fight
for truth, justice and accurate museum exhibits
at Dinamation International Corp.
between 1990 and 1995*

*My bird-brained brethren
of Keane Biological Consulting
who labor by the season
for the good of other species*

*My long-suffering ex-colleagues
who still heave mightily against the inertia
of that oppressive fascist state
that is American public education*

*And, finally, my family –
most importantly
dear Origin and Marion,
beloved Will and Louise
who contributed no less
than flesh and blood
and breath and bone to us...*

www.ingramcontent.com/pod-product-compliance
Lightning Source LLC
Chambersburg PA
CBHW051652040426
42446CB00009B/1098